this soft body

a collection of poems and photographs on coming
home to myself

alysia quinn

also by alysia quinn

the light between the trees
hold her, but let her go

Rising Lotus Press
a division of Rising Lotus Co., LLC
Lakewood Ranch, FL 34202

For more, visit www.alysiaquinn.com
@alysiaquinnpoetry

ISBN: 979-8-218-88445-1

Library of Congress Control Number:
2025926344

Photography & Cover Design by Alysia Quinn

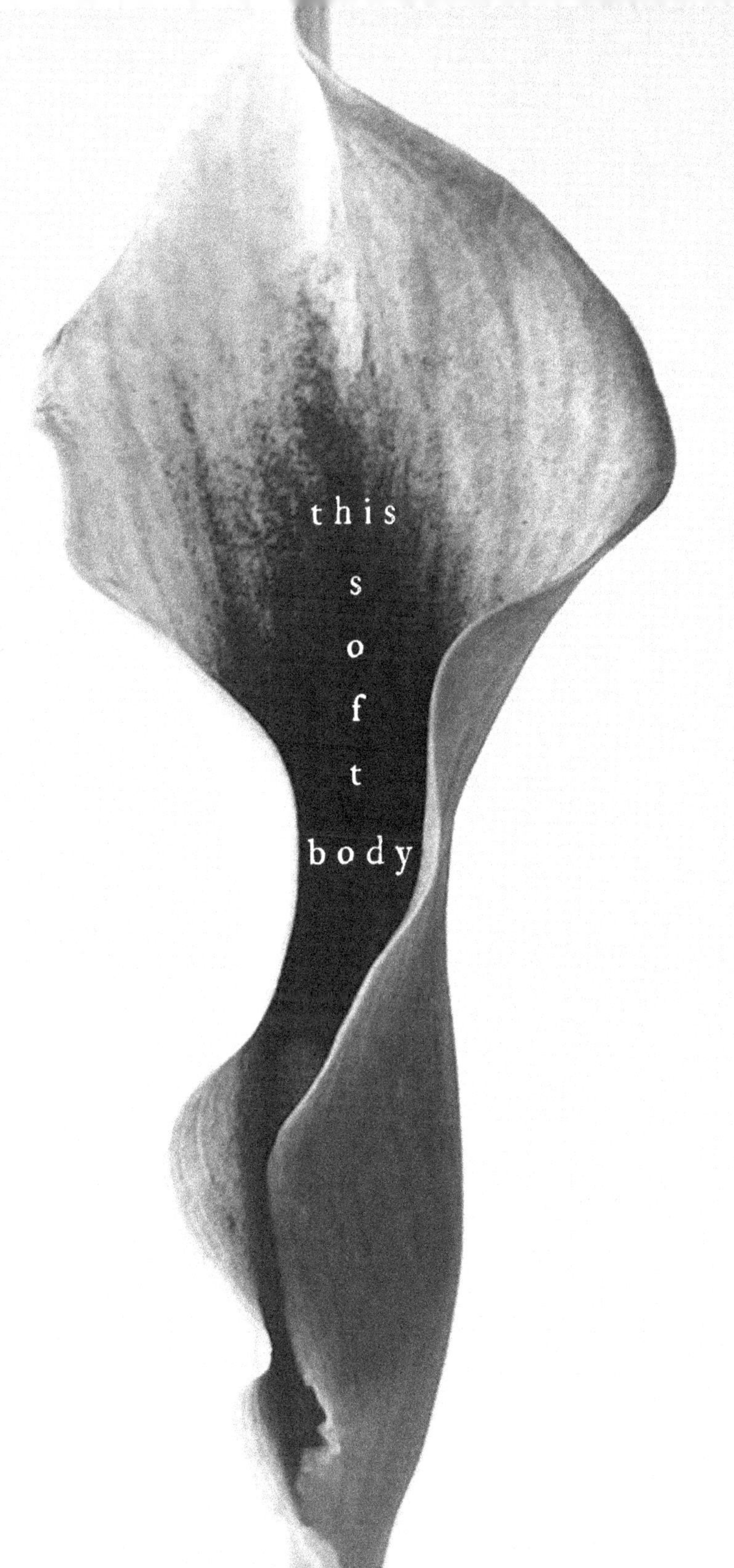

this
s o f t
body

For Jay, in your love and unwavering support. Thank you for being such an incredible witness to my life and for giving me the space to heal and grow. I love you.

For Ethan and Olivia, it is the privilege of my life to be your mom. Thank you for choosing me.

A note from Alysia:

"this soft body" is a collection of writings and photographs I have created on the path of coming home to myself. The process of making art has been a compass on that journey.

As a poet and photographer, the incorporation of visuals you will see here of landscapes, florals, and a few self portraits have felt like the work of presence, ritual, and integration.

This is a collection created as a woman in mid-life. It has been a spiritual process and an ongoing one. It is about my experience with things such as loss, deconstruction, liminality, releasing, unlearning, reordering, reclamation, and embodiment.

The map for the feminine has always been both light and dark, soft and sovereign. We are not only allowed to exist in this space of wholeness, we were created for it.

♡ Alysia

what is left
after the shedding,

but the soft body.

there is a song remembered in the heart,

when we descend
into the darkness,

when we do the work
of reclaiming our soul.

dissolve.

perhaps,

it is the disillusionment phase

of our transformation,

when the outer self

we have built for survival

begins to dissolve,

and we are able to see glimpses

of the soft body —

our true inner being.

not as something

which we must escape

or be rescued from,

but as the very vessel of communion and co-creation

to which we are returning,

where we are held by the friction of our aliveness—

at the intersection of spirit and matter,

where life is remembering and reclaiming, life itself.

your grief is the gate and the guide

on the path of remembering.

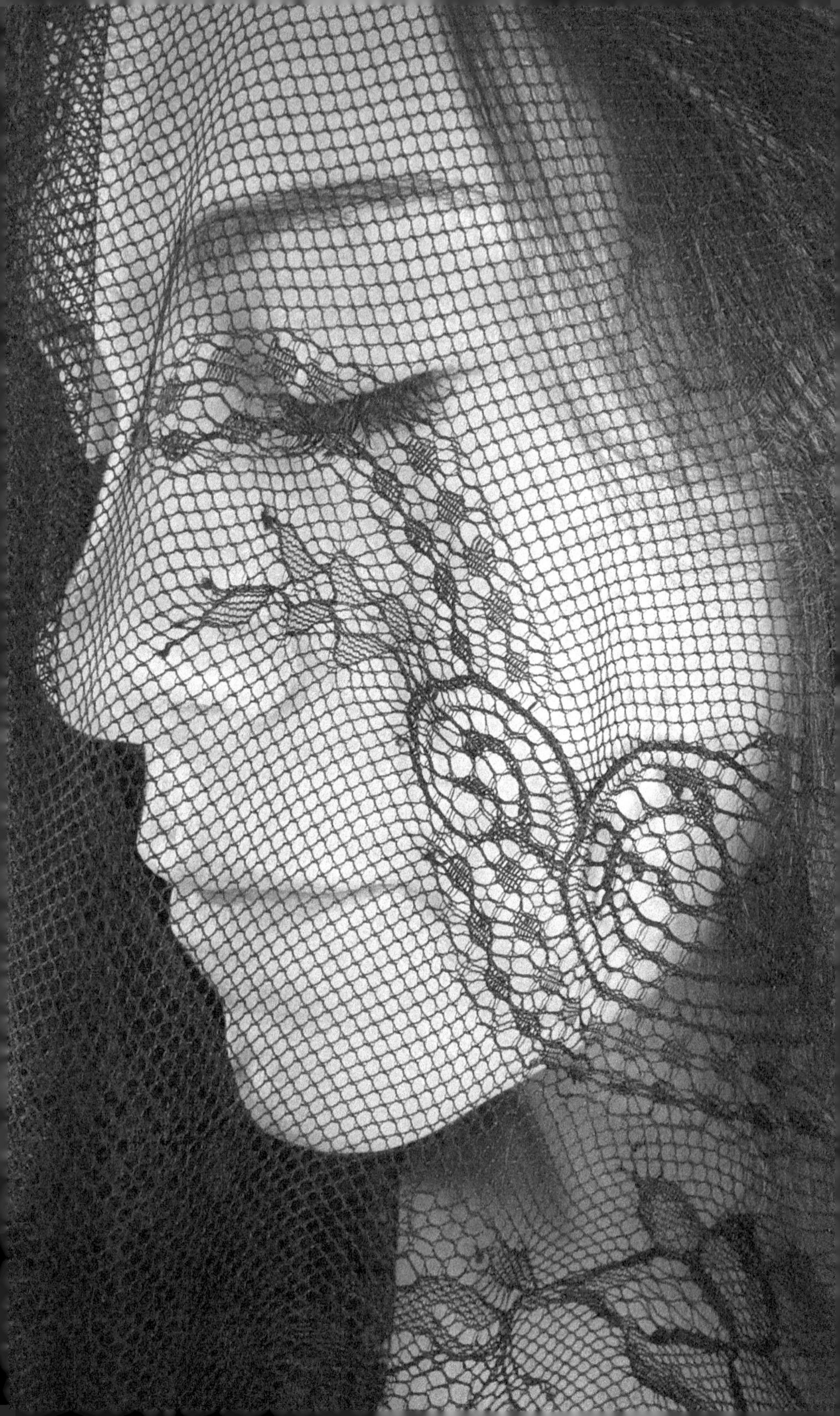

what parts of me have been exiled to survive?
in what ways have i resolved myself
to being only partially known?
what parts are trying like hell to come home?
what have i borrowed from others
and the world to make it this far?
what is mine to carry?
how may i lean into my inadequacies?
how will i courageously lean further
into my gifts?
into my purpose?
into my life?

when all the old constructs
are dismantled,

when i no longer play the old role,

what remains?
what becomes of this letting go?
what becomes of me?

i don't know if i can
see this another way.
can i settle back into my body?
am i gonna be okay?

will i have to start over?

these layers upon layers,
circles inside of circles,

every time i think i heal one thing,
something else comes back up.
i always loved a spiral staircase,
but when is enough, enough?

i guess this death i feel inside
is just a part of being alive,
and maybe, i just want to feel more alive.
maybe, i just want
to feel more—
alive.

and this part

has been about the journey within,

one which has felt more like

a descent—

down to the unknown depths

of where i was told

i should not go—

a deconstructing process

of listening, questioning,

dissecting, dissolving,

reordering, reintegrating,

and returning.

to heal and grow has meant leaving

no stone in my life, unturned.

even and especially, the spiritual ones.

and so, no matter my human failings or frailties,

i continue coming home to this truth—

that Love is the deepest ground i long to walk upon.

and the invitation, as i see it, is to do so here and now,

in this good, soft body.

this body
is a library
of stories —

a lineage of lives
i never lived,
but somehow
ache in my bones.

what was it all for?

how holy
the death cry —
when the veil covers our eyes.

as if anything could separate us
from Love.

there is a part of me
that has always known,

how these things
would always
break my heart,

how grief is the tether—
the unbreakable cord to God,

by which the nourishment
of connection and beauty is received,
as the invitation to remember,
how to love myself back together.

i will always spend time

in the underworld,

in the dark soil of this grief.

this is the work of my garden.

— Persephone

some seasons

are like wombs.

quiet, warm, nurturing—

not meant to keep us,

but to grow us.

to the point where

there is no space left.

where we become

uncomfortable enough

to enter the tunnel of uncertainty,

learning to see in the dark

by feeling our way through

with the changing perceptivity of the heart.

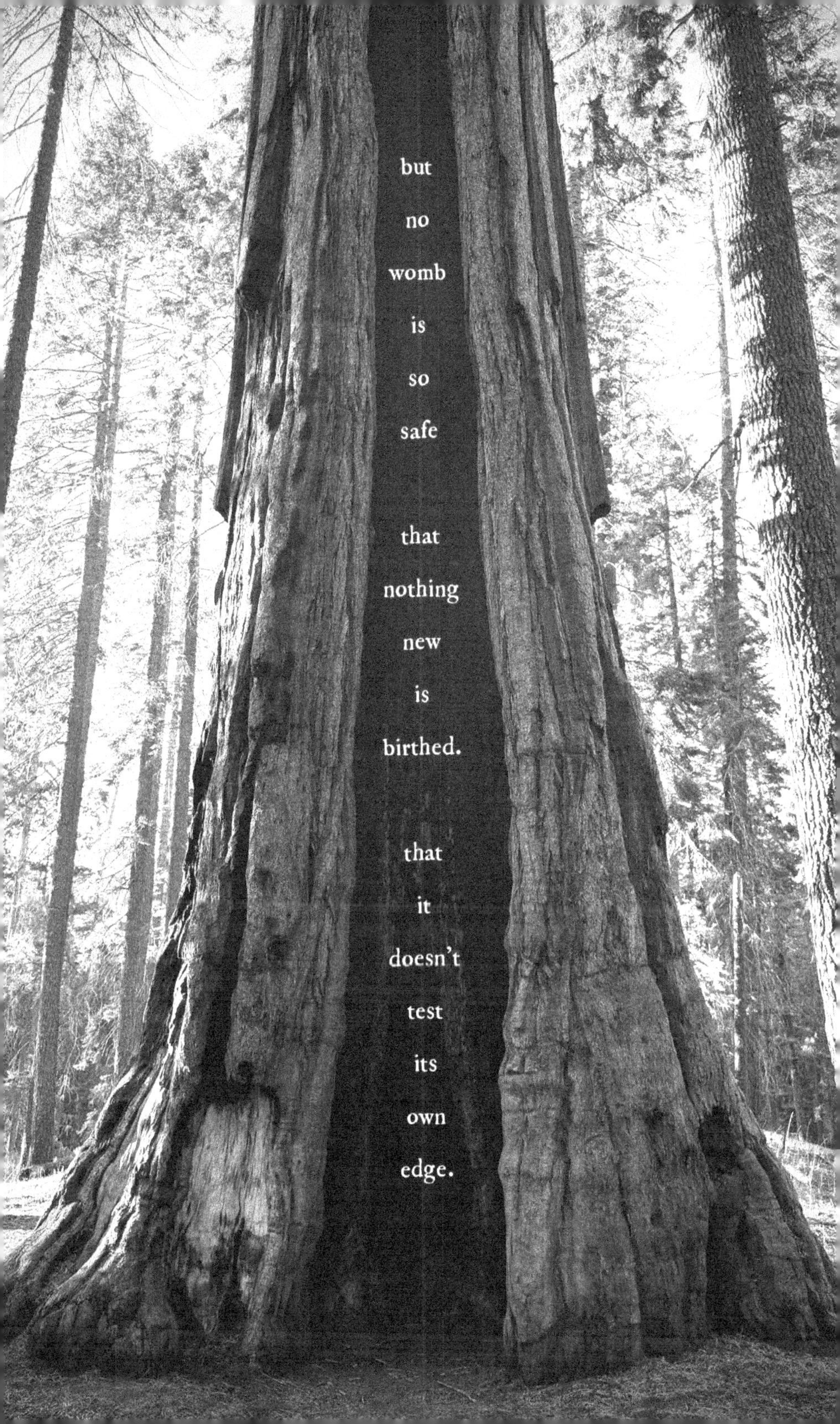
but
no
womb
is
so
safe
that
nothing
new
is
birthed.
that
it
doesn't
test
its
own
edge.

beneath the things like fear and shame,
hides the truth of our deepest heartbreak—

34

heartbreak masked as
busyness, perfectionism, anxiety,
and obsessive productivity.

heartbreak for which
we spend a lifetime
trying everything
not to feel.

amidst uncertainty and despair,
breathes the ache

to be woven together with larger language.
to belong to a bigger story.
to be held in the immensity
of the cosmic current
flowing just beneath
this sorrow—

nothing soaks
a body soft,
like grief.

i haven't had to let
the old versions of me go

as much as i have had
to let them in,

as much as i am learning
how to hold them.

this grief moves

in a harmony of wings,

a murmuration,

keeping warm

in the womb

of the divine infinite sky.

and when it is time,

we are moved into

that space—

even with the squeeze

of reluctance

gripping our insides.

where we remain,

still,

on the edge

of what is dying.

because the potential

for our transformation

lives where the old thing

is held.

these walls are thick
and i cannot see,

but i know —

how darkness demands stillness,
inviting new senses to play.

everything begins in the realm

of the unseen,

in the void space

of silence and seduction.

these wrenching screams
from the center of my being,

i must be slow burning something down.

so i will lay bare
and let the red rain fall.

this place of death.
this place of life.

let the ashes tell the story.
what could be more holy?

an awakened woman is feared
because she will dismantle
everything around her
when clarity arrives in her body.

she knows the storm which rages inside of her
is necessary to bring about her next re-birth
and that her descent into the dark cave
is the initiation.

she knows the doorways
she must pass through
are required for the meeting
of her own void space within,
how her womb is also the tomb.

ask her and she will tell you.

how the birthing process
is the inevitable surrender
to chaos—
a dance with the divine.

where no one comes out
on the other side
the same.

when this pain comes like a wave,

may i inhale and let it.

when it leaves like a tide,

may i exhale and let it.

may i stand on the shoreline,

gazing at the horizon, saying

here i am—

somewhere between

the edge of my human understanding,

and the peace of remembering—

how the wave and the ocean are one in the same,

and i am in the flow of life itself.

the body speaks truths
that the mind was
made to forget.

healing is the practice
of learning
how to listen.

don't tell me this pain
goes away or gets better with time.
it doesn't.
it's just that some days
i figure out how to numb it.

on better days,
i reason with it,
breathe with it,
move with it.

on the best days,
i meet ducklings crossing the road,
i find the light filtering through the trees,
i paint the field in my mind with poppies.

to move out of a state of survival,

and into more awareness,

shines a light upon the shadow.

the healing, which i presumed,

would bring comfort,

seemed to bring complexity.

without the numbing sensations

from distractions, productivity,

old systems of support,

and external validation,

were the reappearing,

underlying questions of

am i enough? for whom?

and by whose standards am i measuring?

because on an even deeper level

of felt understanding,

this part has been about making peace

with my capacity.

with my authenticity.

humility arrives

in the form of

loving presence,

uncovering all of the ways

i have used to survive my pain.

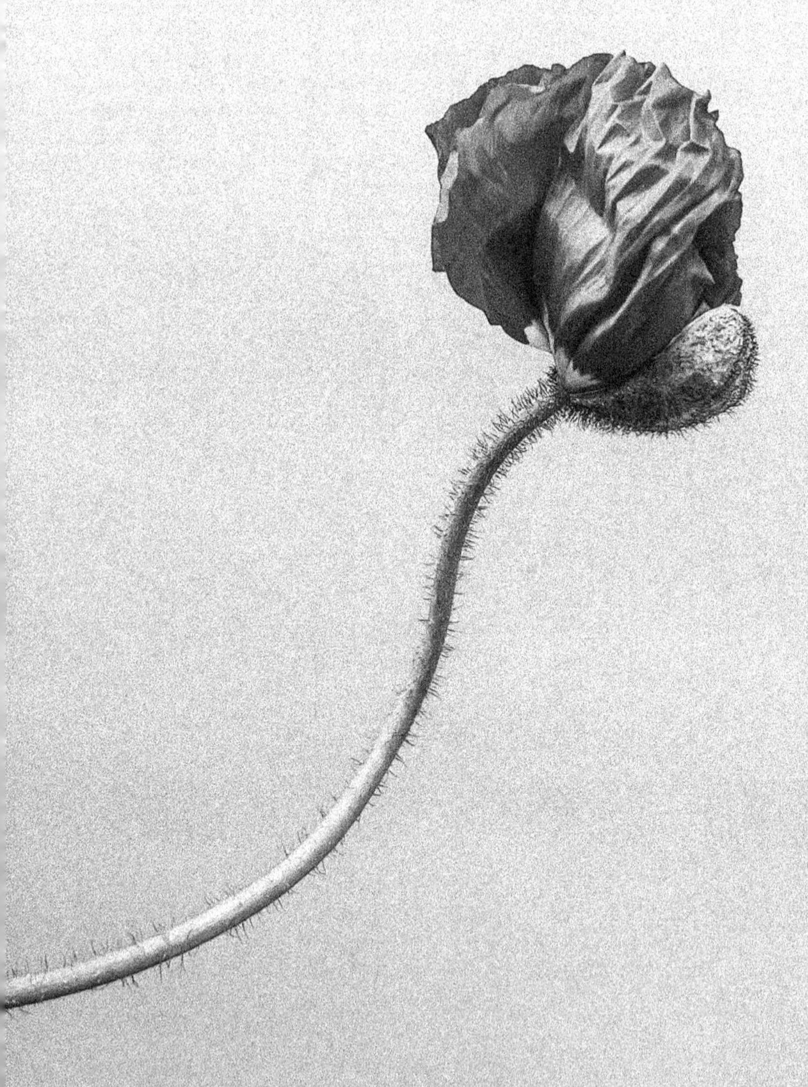

i don't know

if immense beauty

breaks me

or births me,

it feels the same.

i am not sure the word
"uncomfortable"
accurately describes it.

because this part of healing,
this process of integration,

has felt more like the absolute desperation
to be anywhere
but here.

anywhere.
but here.

anywhere.
but.
here.

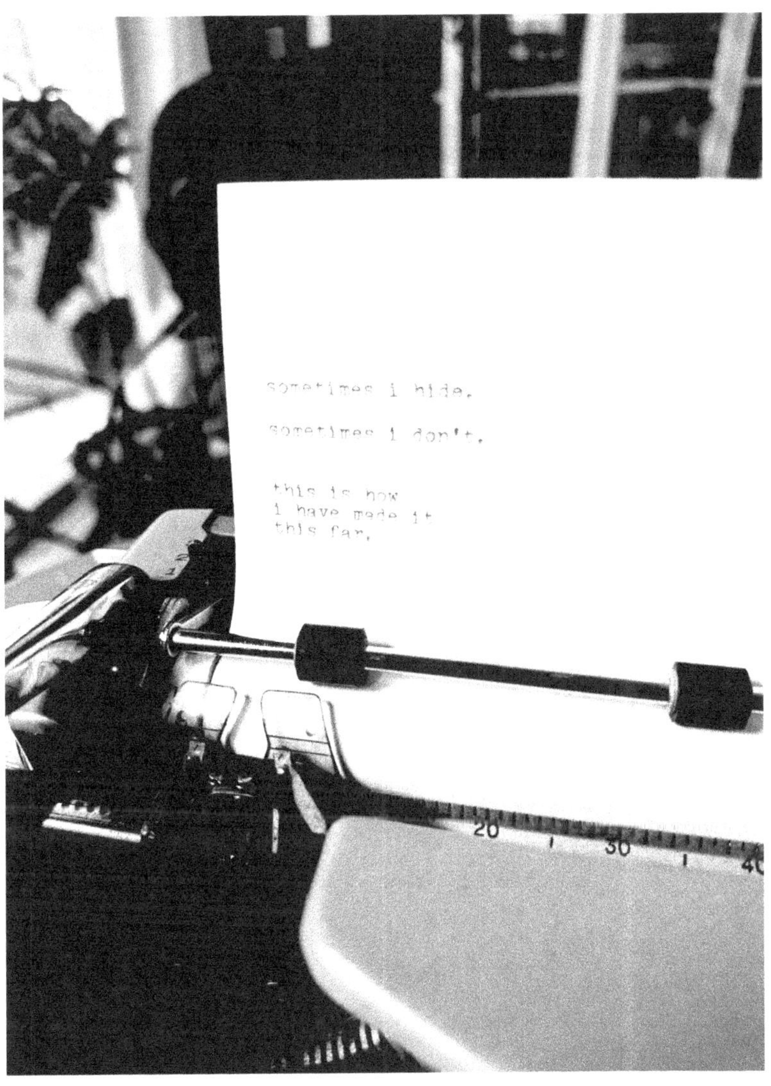
sometimes i hide.

sometimes i don't.

this is how
i have made it
this far,

to grieve is

to not only
befriend uncertainty,
but to know it intimately,

like a soft kiss
on the back of the neck,
unsure as to where
it will all go.

at the end after the end,
at the edge where we think
we have given all we have,

in that death—

lives the magic of lingering.

we speak of the caterpillar
and the butterfly.

but the space between
is where it all happens.

where a body moves
from a lower state
to a higher one,
requiring a disappearance.
so that everything
that once was
is dissolved and dismembered
before it can be
reimagined and remembered,

in the emptiness,
in the field of infinite possibilities.

- Metanoia

sometimes,

beginnings look a lot like endings.

like how seeds
break open
in dark places.

dear earth,
teach me your secrets.
show me how to root
in this darkness,
and re-emerge,
soft and green.

how do i, once again,
breathe in the light?

maybe i will always
struggle with letting in
as much as letting go.

why must my heart
desire to open and close
all at the same time?

the thing about death

is that in some way,
shape or form,
it will bring about
the birth of something new.

and maybe,
one of the most humbling,
devastatingly powerless,
and absolutely gorgeous things
about being alive
is learning
how to hold that tension.

in the dissolution,

remember, this chrysalis still has walls.

even here, there is structure.

even here, in this act of disappearing,

i am contained.

i am safe amidst all of this sorting

because i exist in the underlying truth of being held.

in the messy middle.

in the microcosm of the macrocosm.

in the womb of the imaginal.

you stand at the edge
of beginnings and ends,

what brought you here
was fought for and true
and now the unknown
calls to you

what will you do?

when the hardest thing
to leave behind
is what brought you
to this place.

the bind of my invisibility
was in the ocean of longing
to be deeply seen
nestled beneath
my desire for safety
and protection.

and with that
i assumed the role of
existing between worlds,
mermaid by day,
black cat by night.

somewhere between

the day‑to‑day living in this human experience

and the observations of this human experience

is the story i tell myself.

what happens if i am able

to hold my story, so closely —

that it allows me

to simultaneously

step out of it?

when i don't know

where to go or what to do,

i must remember to get close in.

the closer in i get,

the more i know,

how absence is presence.

nothing can be forced, here.
this phase is for rooting.
for grounding.
for slow walks and
conversations with the trees.
for listening within
when our eyes are unable
to see a way through.

though the ego tries, this is not a time
for winning races or climbing mountains.

while the war wages,
a painter paints, a writer writes, a singer sings.
knowing beauty is the anchor of the soul
and ritual is the ground for presence—
presence required for discernment, for clarity,
and for purpose through which the divine can flow.

tend to the roots.

how do i find meaning
in the suffering
of this life?

what is my own cross to bear?

what if my soul chose this life
and all of its circumstances
to humbly wake me up
to the deepest love?

the internal resistance
the butterfly meets in the darkness
is how she builds her strength.

imagine, love,
the stagnation and frustration you feel
from your internal world not yet aligning
with your external world
is exactly what is necessary
to break out of the chrysalis.

you are becoming the one capable
of holding whatever it is
you have been creating.

as we begin to embody a new shape for a new story,

we do not lose what we started with.

rather, it is carried through

as we transfigure,

as we begin to flow out of ourselves.

deep grief
breaks a person open,
ripens the soft belly of being,
leaves the soil crumbly
and spacious,

inviting the light,
to awaken
the heart,
to a new way of seeing,
for a glimpse into
the true seed of the soul,
the part of us which
can never be taken.

finding the inner child hiding within
means slowing down and becoming curious enough
about why and from whom are they hiding.

finding the true self
underneath of the false self,
requires the guidance
of the inner child.

finding purpose and the deepest meaning
for our lives is not done without
glimpses of the true self.

living into our aliveness
necessitates the integration of all of who we are,
the gifts, the beauty, the flaws, the inadequacies—
compassionately held through practice
by the growing capacity of the person we are becoming.

—Layers

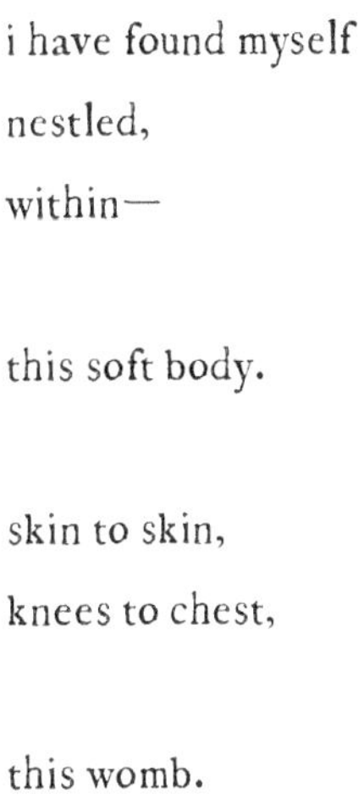

i have found myself
nestled,
within—

this soft body.

skin to skin,
knees to chest,

this womb.
this rebirth.

place your hand on your heart, love.
it is still beating.
never forget, you have a wise heart
within a good body,
a body within The Body,

whatever your story—
it gave you, you.

darling, you are alive,
now,
what will you do?

sometimes, i choose the darkness.
in some ways it feels less frightening

than the courage i know it will take
to walk in the light
of who i am becoming.

the myth of the heroine
depicts the journey within—
WAY down into the depths of hell
and then,
up into the TRUTH of new LIFE—
the baptismal, ever-evolving,
personal and universal patterned process
of bringing what lies in the deep waters
to the surface, where it is held—
and at that very intersection
of heaven and earth,
where the vertical meets the horizontal,
a path is illuminated.
and we discover,
the light has found a way to enter
because of the wound itself.

to really see something,
to understand it,

we must get down
under it.

it is always a path of descent.

there's a good chance
a wound can begin to heal
once we've made contact
with the deepest layer.

rooted inside the rupture,
is the balm we must retrieve,
a medicine made from the bones,
alchemized from the poison
into a salve for the soul and sight.

when everything
we once relied on
has dissolved,

we learn to cope
through the steadfastness
of the loving witness within
or perhaps,
through the compassionate witness
of another person
who has the capacity to help us
remember and return home
to ourselves.

because Love says,
bring it all.
the questions.
the grief.
the mess.

and let us see what is being born.

take notice
of all
that whispers
to you.

perhaps
somewhere,
somehow,
you're calling
your new self
forth.

make your way

towards

all the things

you love.

to love something

is to bring it

to life.

on others

i make magic

from everything

that broke me open.

— ebrah k'dabri (i create as i speak)

sometimes, what we need most
are the little moments
of ordinary beauty,

the ones that feel
safe enough
to hold.

i suppose,

i am a translator of sorts.

something calls me to give shape

to the beauty and truth i encounter.

maybe there is no deeper

form of connection

i long for,

than saying,

i see God here, in this.

do you?

and all at once,

she remembered —

she had grown too civilized

for a girl who spoke

the language of the trees.

remember.

what do we do
with all these
fortress walls
we built for safety?

i am ready
for the light
to kiss my face.

but are you willing

to kiss the parts

of yourself

you find intolerable?

you can
change things
about yourself
WITHOUT being CRUEL
to yourself.
PRACTICING SOFTNESS
will be the way
the LIGHT enters.

it's okay to change.

maybe there is a bind you have

found yourself in,

between the human desire to be seen and loved

and feeling stuck in the loop of performance.

but what if you stopped agreeing

to participate in the performance?

what if you accepted the old truth

that the only constant is change,

not just in the world around you,

but inside of you?

and that a continued devotion of

releasing what isn't you anymore,

over and over,

is what your soul is here for.

because you cannot authentically be you

without losing what you are not.

i am always breaking—

never broken.

there is resistance

involved in remembering.

no matter what we've been through,

before we arrive authentically

to hold hands with the practice

of radical acceptance,

there are dangerous

thresholds to cross

and dragons to be slayed.

the old versions of ourselves

do not go without a fight.

seeing how and wishing
i could've and would've
done some things differently
is in and of itself,
the victory.

growing is the most humbling
thing i've done.

often times,

the things i create or engage with

to support the old version of myself,

eventually become

the cage

for my future self.

which is why it is okay

and necessary

to move on

from things that

i can still consider to be good

in order to move towards

the next things

calling me forward.

i am learning how to let

the soft blue edges

of this rage

emerge from the darkness

to feed it the air

it deserves

this flame is all mine.

she began to hold her rage

as the holy courage

it was—

birthed from the heart

as sacred disruption

with a truer name

called Love.

little girl,
who told you
you had to
smile?

who asked you
to swallow an ocean
of the unspoken
down deep
in your body?

what is the ocean,

if not soft and serene,

intense and full of rage.

this friction i feel

only means
i am alive.

what if there is hardly
any difference between
me and the rose?

what if it is not about searching
for the edge of our fragility,
but remembering our sovereignty?

what if it is about never apologizing
for the way in which we bloom?

every wrinkle

in her petals—

a thousand little

courageous unfoldings.

i shall wait

for the one within

to whisper her secrets.

for she is wild

and she never comes out

when i am looking for her.

everything good

i have made

has been pulled out of

the wet darkness.

for the thrill,
we must tuck her
into the dirt
and let her sleep.

let her be
without the light.

give her space
to endure the breaking.
no restrictions.
no expectations.

how wild
will she emerge?
a rose?
a wolf?
no one knows.

what of this life
is not settling in
to the liminality?
always moving
from what was
to what will be,
when all i have
ever really been
is right here—

on the crest of a wave,
peering over an edge,
standing in a doorway.

this heat you feel is part of the process.

this conflict is worth navigating.

this intensity is what transforms.

and this practice is only about

befriending uncertainty.

it is not about identifying with the opposites,

the good or bad, the joy or pain,

but accepting your wholeness.

let go of how it appears, how you appear.

and no doubt you will, when you begin to see,

how all of this is coming together.

how you are coming together.

by jumping in and learning

how to flow between.

because creating something means

to make order, to shape.

but you must remember

that it comes about

in and through chaos.

—Geronimo

courage begets courage.
instead of suppressing this voice,
it is the work of ongoing healing which
offers the permission,

to listen and pay attention
to the big, uncomfortable questions
i ask in the quiet corners of my heart,
pulling the thread
until the entire veil unravels.

the deepest spiritual truths available
tell us how transformation occurs—

there is no rebirth, without first,
some sort of dissolution or death.

she thought

she was learning

how to dance with

her darkness,

but all along

it was her light.

it was her darkness,

but all along

her light,

how to dance with

she was learning

and she thought

to be washed

in the dark

and sacred waters,

only to arise

skin salty,

bones soft—

baptized by grief.

oh to be ripe and alive.

every time you catch yourself
making yourself smaller,
more camouflaged,
more palatable,

i hope you take a compassionate pause.
i hope you listen for the voice within that says,

i do not have to conform.
i offer myself safety and i can take up space.
i belong.

you are the one

who sees the beauty

143

because the beauty

is you.

shedding the old skin
left you tender and bare,
protecting what is essential within.

what of your soft body
isn't now primed
for expansion?

there is something disruptively stunning about the deconstructing, disorder phase of a woman in mid-life. when she decides, turns, faces, uncovers, leaves—and doesn't look back. when she is on her knees in despair, face-to-face with herself, unveiled. her surrender births a spaciousness, where courage and questions can arise. she learns absence is presence, and an inner knowing becomes her guide. she creates boundaries with smaller circles, disengaging from systems and dogma. she watches her old beliefs die, while her faith in a mystery, expands. she listens less to the external world, and more to the quiet voice within. her expression becomes her prayer. her rebellion, her reclamation. her love, a sacred disruption. she remembers she is made of oceans and stars. she reclaims her wholeness. and she begins to return herself, to herself.

every time

you encounter an edge,

standing less clothed

at the cusp of something new,

at the doorway of your next steps,

you will be misunderstood.

wake up.

forget the plot.

howl.

i am always somewhere between—

this call to wander
and
this pull to put down roots,

which i can see are just
two sides of the same prayer—

a longing for the resonance
only felt in one's heart,
for the sound of beauty,
for the song of home.

what if this life
is a dream
from which
i am waking?

what if the land
calling me home
is found
in the sacred landscape
of this soft body?

what is this heartache
i carry for a place
i call home?

i have spent an awfully long time
trying to get there.

perhaps, the secret lies
in the soft openings.

in the poem and the purr,
in the peach and the posy,
in the prayer of Clair de Lune.

find your way to that place.
then, close your eyes
and wait patiently
for instructions.

come find me.

the darkness is the initiation
and the body is the map,

157

for the profound journey
taken from the head to the heart.

if the heart
is where beginnings
and endings meet,

then home is right here —

where strong meets soft,
where laughter meets tears,
where inhale meets exhale.

you are learning

to let go

by sitting just a little while longer

each time

in the discomfort —

holding the tension

between two things.

it may feel counterintuitive,

but wisdom says

something new will arrive.

and the way you must go

will be revealed.

there are many paths of becoming,

many ways the light will play,

many kinds of beautiful,

many shades of gray.

in the immense death
of what is perceived
as lost,
also lives all of your
new beginnings.

this is what
the artist in you
inherently knows.

164

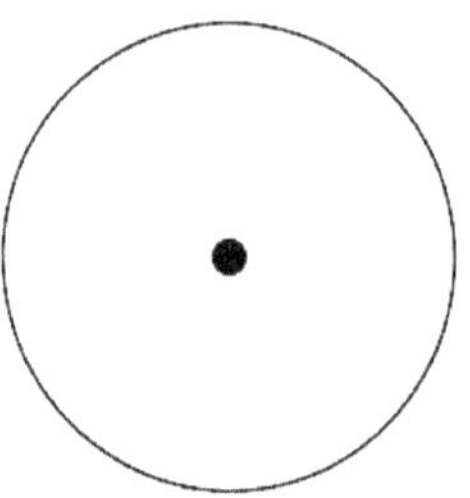

how do we know

when we have reached

the bottom—

the darkest part

of the journey?

we don't.

and perhaps

that is the point—

the point at which

we surrender, again and again,

to something larger

than ourselves.

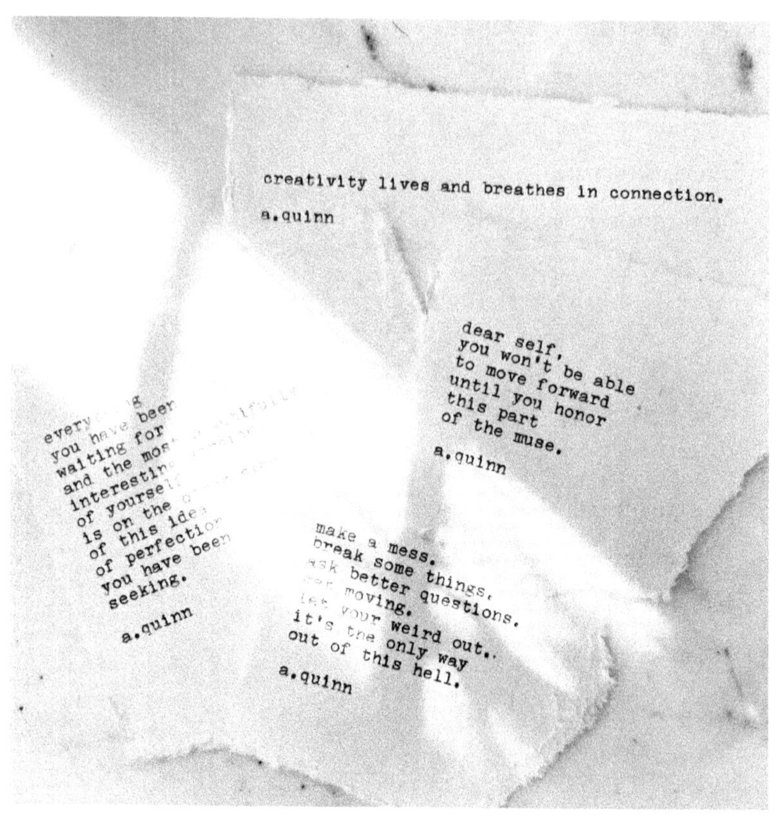
creativity lives and breathes in connection.

a.quinn

dear self,
you won't be able
to move forward
until you honor
this part
of the muse.

a.quinn

every
you have been
waiting for
and the most
interesting
of yourself
is on the
of this idea
of perfection
you have been
seeking.

a.quinn

make a mess.
break some things.
ask better questions.
moving.
let your weird out.
it's the only way
out of this hell.

a.quinn

may you honor

the part of you
who in the hopeless moment
asked for help.

the part of you
who in the darkest time
decided to create.

the part of you
who in the loneliest hour
offered yourself enough safety
to risk belonging
for authentic expression
and connection.

grief is processed
through both
feeling and expression.

as we create,
we heal.

the inner child awaits
for our return
at the gate of the garden.

the younger part of us,
so connected with source,
invites us into more of who we are
by remembering the rhythm of our being,
inhaling inspiration through play
and exhaling whatever is ours to create.

and like a return to breath itself,
it soon becomes unclear
if we are the ones making the art
or if the art is making us.

to live in service
of the soul

is to sing the song,
already written,
waiting to be discovered,
on the inside of your heart.

rivers and stars,
water and dust,

what of her is not
flowing and finding
creating and shining.

we connect and make,

mend and break.

over and over,

finding our way home

to ourselves

and each other.

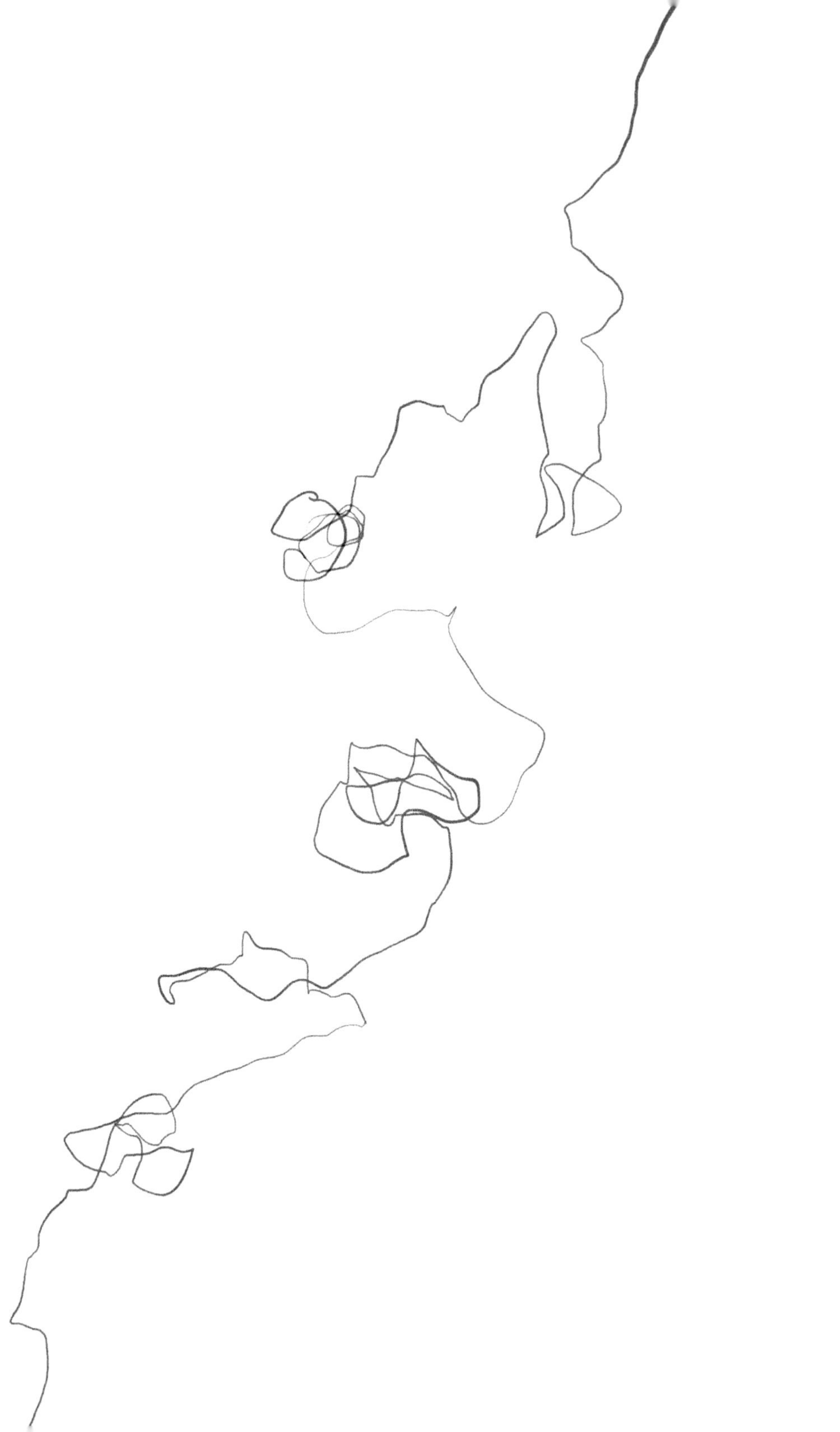

it is a slow unraveling

to unpack with care,
the deep pain we hold
in our bodies,
consciously and
unconsciously
within our stories,
shifting out of the past
and into the space
of the present moment.

with kindness and curiosity,
we can follow the thread.

when my mind searches endlessly
for answers to feel more in control,
my heart whispers,
how the only way home
is to walk the path

a little bit lost.

the holding

of my own
humanness,

of all the ways
i have been
unable
to show up

is the way forward.

what has cost you,

will catapult you.

what has darkened your doorway,

will illuminate your gifts.

if tended to with care,

the wound becomes the work,

your sacred offering to the world.

an old story of shame

repeats a pattern of scarcity,

where productivity

and performance

attempt to cure

the deep underbelly

of not - enough - ness.

but what if that story

was written in the sand,

only to be rewritten

by sitting in the current within —

the current revealing

the truer story

in your growing soul.

— Father Wound

if something feels
not quite right
about whatever it is
we may be choosing
or creating,
being able to say

this isn't it

may be one of
the most courageous
things we do.

because of old stories,

sometimes it is hard

for me to remember

that what i make or do

is not who i am,

but the road i am walking

and trusting

will bring me home.

your light will disrupt, let it.
your light will trigger others, let it.

perhaps, your light made you
a target for envy as a child—
even by those considered closest to you.
so, it makes sense that hiding your light
back then was the safest place to live.

and now you're here.
you can hold this now.
do the work to uncover yourself.

your light will disrupt, let it.

what if this longing,

the longing in our hearts
we have been told
to deny or suppress,

is the very prayer itself?

what if the practice
of this prayer
leads us down the path
of remembering—

our wholeness,
our inner witness,
our inherent goodness,
our divine spark within.

you must take a step in,

so that you may take

a step out.

your becoming

is both outward

and inward.

there is no way

around it,

only through it.

the world is waiting

for you to claim

who you are.

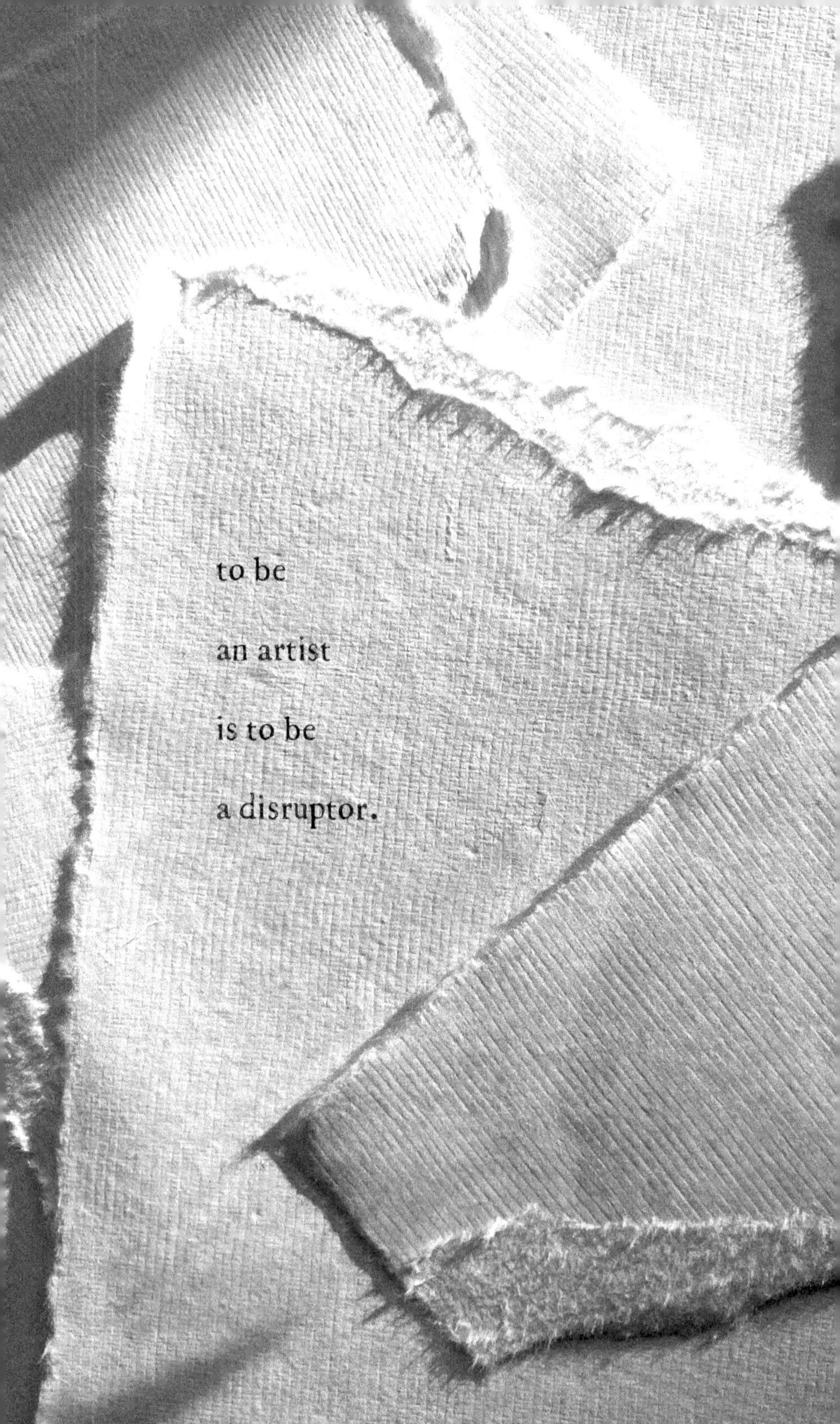
to be

an artist

is to be

a disruptor.

to create

requires friction,

a force of one thing

wearing

fraying

resisting

polishing another.

encountering an edge offers

a transfer of energy.

like light to seed,

breath to wave,

spirit to matter.

there is magic
to be found
in the daily devotion
of finding ways
to open yourself up
to your own life.

look for the portals.

the less we need to be right,

the more interesting our art becomes.

192

the more interesting

everything becomes.

any discipline
involves the meeting
of resistance within.
and in that friction
lives the possibility
of a shift in the intention—

from force to surrender,
from discipline to devotion—

the opening to the space
in which love freely flows.

the way forward

always seems like it is

about learning how

to be

right where

i am.

maybe, this aching for
a forever home
begins with
a forever door—

an invitation, ever-present and hidden,
in the participation with this life,

an invitation into the deep waters of grief,
where loss comes to be named and known,
not as less painful,
but as the pathway
to a richer, resurrected life.
a pathway no one can take for us,
that appears when we are ready,

with a forever door—

always there. always within.
waiting to be walked through.

inside of me

lives

a wise woman,

reminding me

she unfolds

for no one,

but herself.

soon it became apparent

that if integration was the goal,

then her path would

look different from his.

her path would be

to first develop and hold

the parts of herself

she was told from the beginning

were either too much

or not enough.

because how can a woman

let go of

that which she has not

fully held?

what if the night sky
is a reflection of you?

did you know you are made of stars?

maybe that is what you are doing, love,
with all those scattered specks of light—

you're reclaiming your wholeness,
by dancing with the dark.

it may take some time
and grief to see it,
but there is an unfolding happening
within you.

no matter what you may think
in the quiet moments of your mind,
you do not need to be ahead
of where you are,
nor can you go back.
you haven't missed it.
feel your regrets all the way through
and allow them to guide you.
you are precisely where
you need to be.

i wonder who

i might have become

without all these heavy

things i carry?

i wonder who

i am becoming

because of them?

a.quinn

embody.

once she remembers

and begins to experience

her own light,

she must learn to

tend it,

carry it,

and protect it.

so it can emerge in the way

it was always meant to —

as the flame and the wildfire,

as the soft breast and the strong back,

as a woman who knows the truth

is in the legs themselves

and between her own.

matter.

mater.

mother.

maybe,

the most stunning thing

a woman gives birth to

is herself.

over and over,

again.

every layer of this body
holds an earlier version of myself
that survived — then stepped aside,

all to bring this current version to life.

after a series of cracks,

it is the profundity of this shift

that shakes the foundation,

when she finally asks herself,

what actually matters here for me?

what do i want?

how are we to know
the highest expression
of anything or anyone?

nurture the space for spirit.
allow for the unfolding.

to cross over this threshold
into midlife

214

is to claim
not only my story,
but my sovereignty.

it is to claim
the longing of my soul.
to live more deeply and fully
in this body.

to be with her

in any real way,

you must learn

the language of the trees,

the way of sacred exchange.

where the breath

only rises if it roots

in safe space,

where your hallow

meets her vibration.

man, don't you know?

she's the sound of your kingdom.

a woman's lungs were made to howl.

how fascinating to see
how things are hidden
in plain sight,
how the mysteries unfold
as we do.

how we can
re - visit,
re - listen,
re - read
something,

only for it to reveal
it was there
the whole time.
it never changed.
we did.

don't forget how they split us

into virgins and whores,

when we've always been both.

but i suppose

it's understandable

as to why.

a woman in her fullness

has always been a threat.

— The Thing About The Marys

contrary to what we can

inherit as women,

honoring this body

never meant abandoning it,

but learning how to

notice and live more fully

on the inside of it —

declaring with the whole of ourselves

that the world's expectations

for the feminine

to soften, open, and receive,

can only be authentic

if we also get to

demand, desire, and devour.

i am experiencing
the fullness of life
in all of its heartbreak and joy.

i am experiencing
the fullness of life.

i am experiencing.

i am.

if we know dissolution precedes solution
in the alchemical process.

then we can begin

to notice and name

that when we are returned

to the darkness,

personally or collectively,

we can hold onto the wisdom

which tells us that solutions

can still be revealed

but in ways

the old version of ourselves

cannot yet see.

she who is awakened

does not chase,

225

but enters her own

deep waters,

magnetizes,

and receives.

aliveness arrives,

often by surprise,

in the unfolding

of our own personal myth.

there is a life i used to live,
too small for me now.

and i have become a stranger
to that world,
to those who used to know me,

what a curious mix of feelings—

to be so lonely,
and yet,
more myself
than ever before.

maybe she's a catholic. or a baptist. or a new age freak. or a self-proclaimed goddess with a body washed in tattoos that remind her who she is. or maybe she's a crystal loving weirdo, into chakras, astrology, and mythology. or a yogi whose altar holds a Buddha statue beside her Jesus and Mary Magdalene ones. maybe she meditates to chanting monks and an aramaic version of The Lord's Prayer. or maybe she's a crunchy, sign-seeing, pattern-recognizing prophet who finds God in the trees and mountains more than anywhere else. or maybe she's a rainy-day-when-everything-is-shit, atheist. or a bible idol-ing good girl who writes scripture on her bathroom mirror, including the lines from the gospels they left out. maybe she's lost. maybe she's not. maybe she goes to a church once in a while. or maybe not.

or maybe she's a feminist, f*ck the patriarchy, burn it all down type. or a body worshipping slut. or virgin. or an artist who knows the only thing worth doing is living into a divine mystery with her whole body and a messy practice of expression. maybe she's a seeker with enough courage to ask the questions most deny having. maybe all the suffering does that — you know — maybe it breaks the heart open so much that surrender is the only option left. maybe she knows — this is how it works — that surrender arrives right before Love rides through a wildfire on a white horse named Grace — to bring it all back together again. maybe she knows God made her to be all of these things. on purpose. loved. whole. free. for a time such as this.

grief didn't just make
a home in this chest—

it carved a lair.

for the woman
who would emerge
on the other side
of that pain.

as i dig into my spiritual tradition,
these roots grow deeper each day.
and i get the sense
that the highest form of faith
i can embody is

to embrace the mystery.
to follow the trail of frankincense.
to open my heart through a practice
to the song of the divine.

one day, the Goddess called to me through a photograph i had taken. felt as an inner pull, a sort of whisper to mark the event, i wrote a quick poem down in my notebook that included the word "Goddess," which at the time, made me uncomfortable. and curious. she kept calling to me in many different ways — in signs and songs, in conversations and nature, in synchronicities. some felt like love letters and others like painful truths in shattered picture frames. but all were pointing me towards being able to see my story in hers.

over time, i realized mythology would be a doorway in my heart i could walk through into more self-exploration and healing. because myths are fictional stories, except with the greatest underlying, universal truths. in them, we find archetypes gifting us with words mirroring our own journeys, the stories of humanity to which we belong, and the permission and inspiration for meaning-making, creative expression, and play.

eye to eye,

crowns to scars,

in reverence and rhythm,

in the heart's recognition.

there she appeared,

the Goddess,

in a field of gold.

this season is asking you to trust it.
to put your feet on the ground, right here.

to step into your courage
and claim your humanness,
by slowing down to listen.

to open yourself to the invitation
calling to you from your heart.

to move your body
in a true kind of way—
in a soft, full belly,
here - one - minute - not - the - next,
boots, barefoot, hair wild,
you decide,
kind of way.

Love is the witness
we spend a lifetime
in search of.

only to find it has been
within
this whole time.

maybe then,

the invitation

is here and now,

to live into

this body.

perhaps, the most loving thing
you can do today
is nothing.
the kind of nothing
that is everything.

let yourself be
where you are.

you could've remained in that pattern of reacting. and you wouldn't have necessarily been wrong. reacting to circumstances became a way of life— a way you survived hard things. things that harmed you. things that shaped you in ways you're still learning to see and overcome. things you've had to deeply grieve and repair within and for yourself. and perhaps the most interesting part of doing all that tedious, internal work is that somewhere along the way instead of reacting to the pain caused each time, you've gained the power to choose your next steps, thoughtfully. you've come to understand— you have agency. you've come to the awareness of radical acceptance. and that kind of power feels overwhelming and even frightening. because now, having the power to choose holds you responsible. and this is a shift— a letting go. a reclaiming. this is where the new version of yourself bows to the old version and says, thank you for bringing me this far. this is where the new version of yourself says to the old version, your work is finished, i will take it from here— i will trust myself. i get to choose.

it is worth closing your eyes,

and envisioning your final earthly breaths,

to notice how the greatest heartbreak

you could experience

would be the heartbreak

of your own self-abandonment.

what is it you need

in order to live deeply

into your aliveness?

whatever it is
you are looking for,

it's already yours.

to see the light is because

we have seen shadow.

to live is to also have

a contract with death.

and in the dual nature

of things in this realm,

separation seems to be both

the requirement and the illusion

by which we come to know

and be known.

at the root,

the spiritual traditions tell us

all is well. all is whole. all is one.

and the gift we have been given

by God to discover this

is relationship itself.

the more i acknowledge uncertainty,

inviting sorrow to soften the edges of my heart,

the nearer i sense the presence of divine immensity,

which somehow speaks to me in a language all my own.

perhaps, this is the rhythm of the holy,

a conversation i am having within and with the world,

both particular and universal,

like a quiet hum, just under the breath,

communion with creator and creation,

a sacred dance of synchronicity,

a murmuration.

maybe, the birds
have collected
each of their feathers,

a body
of work,
a soul
of lifetimes.

embodied enough
to sing their song
in harmony with all
of creation.

the truth is, the treasure

is what we find

within,

when we are ready

to stop hiding

ourselves from ourselves.

when we are ready

to claim

what is already ours

leading us to ask,

how much courage

do we have

to face our shadow?

how much beauty

can we bear?

if creating is about process.
and the process is what brings presence.

whether time is a thief or an illusion.

then practicing presence
is what we have.

and our art,
however we define it

is how we do it.

how we make
~~a living.~~

a life.

i hope you follow
that silly little impulse
that tells you to make or create.

you know,

that voice without words
that keeps asking you.

to paint,
or write,
or...

what if it's a waste of your time?
what if it's not?
what if it makes you happy?
what if taking a chance on yourself
changes your life?
what if everything you actually want
is on the journey of making
whatever art is yours to make?

the loss of innocence

can gift us wisdom,

and one day,

wisdom gifts us back

our innocence.

as we heal,

the cynic within

is set free,

only to reveal

we are becoming

the artist.

with enough felt safety,

we begin the work

of coming face -to -face

with our deeper fears,

learning how

to extend invitations

rather than answers.

every time
we make our art

255

we reclaim

our power.

we must do what

we need to do

in order to let go

so that we are able

to enter a world of imagination.

or we will keep trying

to live out an old story

that simply cannot be lived out

from this place,

from these new versions of ourselves.

we must be brave enough

to let the whole thing crumble,

surrendering to the emptiness required,

for the birth of something new.

while we may be blinded

in the moment,

we have the capacity

to look back and see things

more clearly.

maybe, the soul agrees

to this plan

long in advance,

to bring about

whatever is necessary

for the expression

of the highest self,

remembering the old song

imprinted on our hearts.

the best people i know
have taken the broken pieces
of their lives and used them
to create something new
and beautiful,

but not before

those sharp edges
left them bleeding,
blind, powerless,
and breathless.

we should normalize telling others
how in awe of them we are

for finding such beautiful ways
to alchemize their pain.

to write

what cannot

be fully written.

to photograph

what cannot

be fully photographed.

to sing

what cannot

be fully sung.

the beauty of art

is birthed

in our attempts

to name the unnamable.

the most sacred blessings come

when we choose to embrace

the gifts we've been given

by using them to create

what is ours to create

before we think we are ready.

whatever it is we decide

to bring forth,

whatever it is we touch

with our love,

our offering will send out ripples,

far past what we can see.

we cannot know the reach of our arms.

her power was not
that she had
the sharpest of claws
or the softest touch,

but in her evolution
of learning how to be
present enough
in each moment
to discern which one to use.

in time, we come to learn
that negative space
is the emptiness required
for infinite possibilities.

and the task
is not to work harder
trying to fill that space,
but rather to let go
of whatever we must
in order to create that space.

disobeying

the good girl within

becomes the threshold

necessary to cross,

in order to move from

maiden to mother,

and to ask the truer questions

the inner wild feminine

longs to ask.

when the old narrative she was handed

can no longer bear the weight,

nor offer the space,

to the woman who knows she is more,

she is confronted with the way of things.

with the truth that what had formed her

was now ready to let her go.

as is the nature of wombs.

—Ode to Eve

while the world
says otherwise,

something deep inside
tells her,

that this is
her most beautiful season.

somewhere along the way,
the battle with this body ceased.
i cannot tell you when,
only that it did.

only that i find myself
sitting in the middle of this bustling cafe
not with that old familiar tension,
but with a slow breath, soft middle.

only that this tall frame which could never hide,
isn't trying to anymore,
but is instead adorned
with a silky, bold bandana.

only that this damp hair drips,
long, washed, and wavy,
without demands
of perfection or performance,
wildly finding the way—
like the river that only knows how to flow free,
like a woman who decided to let herself be.

peace after healing
is going back
to the old place
with new eyes.

this grief brings a longing for another garden,
another place that might cure this ache.

but i wonder if i may hold on
for just a little while longer?

there are bits of green
showing through this earth,
right here.

i wonder if everything
in this garden
is about to bloom?

i will bloom
because i am ready.

otherwise, i will only wither.

i will reap this season
for which i am ripened.

for if i do not,
i may find it impossible
to reap any season at all.

the pain of life

allows us to make the turn

inward, beyond the mind.

and with openness,

we receive ears to hear

and sight from the heart,

seeking and finding

the sovereignty within,

on the road of spiritual surrender.

— The Path of Paradox

it has been my experience
that there is no healing
without God.

and that as i change and expand,
so does my perception of the divine.

—Abwoon

when it feels as though

i am stripped

of my power,

i am guided by ritual.

it is ritual

that offers agency,

ground for alchemizing

pain into beauty.

and through the essence

of that beauty,

i can remember who i am.

this river of intensity
was always yours.
let your heart beat
and your eyes weep.

feel and flow
unapologetically.

this time,
i will not let
the uncertainty
drown me.
i will swim
in its depth
and trust
in its tide.

a.quinn

wherever you are,

whatever you are learning

or unlearning,

whoever you are becoming

or unbecoming,

bring that.

bring your conversation,

however you will,

offer that to the world.

roots run red,

branches that bind,

all these pieces of myself

i had to find.

and there in the midst

of all my deaths,

a home i built inside.

—I See a Tree

on an ordinary day,

i look up to see

ten‑thousand starlings, mid‑air,

whispering truth, as bodies do—

not with words,

but with the chest‑felt vision

of wonder and unity.

where the idea of separateness

becomes illusory and the message

received in the heart

is something more than

the sum of its parts,

witnessed in a sky symphony of birds,

shape‑shifting into songs of sacred geometry,

a sensation i can only name as God.

every now and then,
run your fingers
across the scar.

remind yourself
how far you've come.

i hope you look back
on your life and remember
everything you've been through,
survived through,
thrived through,
to get here.

it has not been easy,
but you were never made for easy.
you were made to disrupt,
to remember who you are,
and to share your light.
you were made for more
and deep down inside
you know this to be true.
so, keep going.
bet on yourself.

early on, when the pain of life became too much and the grief was too great to manage alone, disconnection from the body was not a choice, but survival. in our human need for connection, we learned that in order to get through life, we must construct a protective shell, searching outside of ourselves for validation, comfort, and meaning. and we either walk that path until we die — or until we reach the end of it by means of some sort of suffering, here in this body, where we begin to awaken by looking within. we learn how to offer ourselves safety, remember how to use our voice, how to feel again, how to keep our grief warm, how to slow down, and eventually how to allow ourselves to be seen again through the dissolving and breaking of that shell. we learn by experience that the magic of healing lies in being compassionately witnessed in our pain, discovering we are no longer alone in it. this is the love that heals. this is the love that replaces our self-contempt with self-compassion. and from that place, we have what is necessary to walk across a threshold where we begin to release, receive, and return. where we come home to ourselves.

when a woman

comes home

to herself,

she doesn't come home

empty-handed.

she returns with medicine.

the truth is,

at first and for a while,

it is lonely and messy

and maybe the bravest thing

you will ever do.

to love yourself

back to gether.

a. quinn

these tears of ours

were made for falling.

this softness, not weakness,

but the merciful flow of the river itself —

not from us, but through us,

a powerful force

bending the banks of soil and time —

pouring itself out

into the current,

and like you and me,

it is how the river remembers

the way to the sea.

and finally,

all the versions of her

returned and knelt

in the garden.

seeds sensuously wrapped,

nourished in the blanket

of all her shedded skins.

a golden warmth felt

in the landscape

of her soft body,

a reclamation,

ripe for union.

a knowing,

remembered in her heart.

with her palms prayerfully pressed,

and her petals powerfully crowned,

her two-lips apple red.

she was naked and unashamed.

—Garden Goddess

she held all
of the contradictions
of her life.

the way the night sky
holds the stars.

i am.

the garden of velvet flesh petals,

the circle of trees with roots and rhythms,

the shedding slither with fangs of destruction,

the soil which nourishes and cradles the mountains.

the fierce inner flame, alchemical, undimmable,

the sacred womb, weaver of waves,

the cosmic lullaby, the priestess portal,

and the moonlight that fades.

impermanent.

immanent.

daughter.

divine.

i am

w (om) an

i descend.

i arise.

whatever blooms from these bones,

may it be— of love,

may it be from choosing to live

more fully into the rhythms of my seasons,

where rest is not feared as weakness

and productivity does not equal worth.

with awareness of how the

external reflects what is internal.

may it be a slow hymn of surrender,

courageously giving the necessary parts

of me permission— to die or to bloom.

may it be in removing weeds from tender wounds

and planting seeds in holy darkness.

may it be from prayers of strength,

patiently waiting for the light.

may it be because the weight of grief

breaks the temple of my heart wide open —

and there in the silence, revealing the sacred,

hallowed place within,

the place where gardens grow.

— Nethqadash Shmakh (Hallowed Be Thy Name)

to have a mother wound is to be disconnected from the body. and we

walk towards healing

because we cannot build a world with soul,

without roots.

we cannot build something worthy

of our children and their children,

while disconnected from our own feminine energy.

from the womb of the earth.

from the soil of Her body.

from the unseen void space where creation and destruction occur.

in a time where everything is analyzed

and logically rationalized,

but not felt and sensed,

we must remember

a tree reaches and rises, but not without its roots

growing down, deeper.

to return home

you must place your feet
upon the mat.
allow the sound of welcome
to flow all the way up
into the chambers of your heart.

you must ask and knock
on the door of blessing.

and then perhaps,
the most difficult part,

you must learn
how to tolerate standing there,
in all your new bareness.

to receive what has always
been yours.

Alysia Quinn is an artist whose work speaks of healing, grief, trauma, and the path of self-discovery. It is her mission to share her authentic voice and story through creative writing and photography. She hopes that her work offers a source of encouragement, strength, meaning, and beauty to those walking a healing path.

for more, visit www.alysiaquinn.com

@alysiaquinnpoetry